MAKING KNITWEAR FIT

MAKING KNITWEAR FIT

Pat Ashforth
&
Steve Plummer

Janet Pownell

GUILD OF MASTER CRAFTSMAN PUBLICATIONS

First published in this form in 1996 by
Guild of Master Craftsman Publications Ltd
166 High Street, Lewes
East Sussex BN7 1XU

© Pat Ashforth and Steve Plummer 1996

ISBN 1 86108 022 0

Diagrams by Pat Ashforth
Sketches by Steve Plummer

Designed by Fineline Studios

Typeface: Minion

Printed and bound by Redwood Books Ltd, Trowbridge, Wiltshire

Contents

Introduction

Getting knitwear to fit properly is not a matter of luck, nor is it a major mathematical challenge. It relies on common sense and simple calculations.

The most skilful knitter in the world will rarely produce perfect results by following a pattern blindly, and yet many people are put off adapting patterns or creating their own designs because it seems difficult. It is not hard if you know what you need to do and why you need to do it.

This book aims to give you a logical, easy-to-follow approach to altering or designing knitwear patterns. It is mainly about how to carry out the calculations you need to get started. Its companion volume, *Creating Knitwear Designs*, explains some of the more creative decisions in greater detail, but in the same systematic manner. It is impossible to separate the practical and aesthetic aspects of design completely, so some topics appear in both books, with different emphasis.

There is nothing here about knitting techniques. There is nothing about your artistic talents as a designer, or about choice of yarns or colours. It is entirely about the calculations you need to do to make something fit.

Some of the information here could be considered very basic, but getting the basics wrong is the downfall of many knitters. If you need to go back to first principles, then this book is for you. It shows you how to measure a tension square without assuming that you must have done it before – but it does not stop there. You will eventually progress to solving simultaneous equations before you can knit a sleeve. 'I'm no good at maths,' did you say? Lack of confidence is often more of a problem than lack of ability. You *can* manage these calculations – with the help of a calculator. Get them right, and your new sweater will fit.

Kangarule is not the sort of jumper we are really interested in, but she is useful to have around because she carries all the essentials in her pocket – measuring equipment, calculator, pencil and paper. Joey is often in there too, and can be rather demanding at times.

Note

The examples in this book give metric measurements only, in the interests of clarity (except for the tension calculations on pages 9–20). They are there simply to demonstrate principles and the rules are the same whether you work in imperial or metric. For your own calculations, you can use whichever units you prefer. For an easy way to convert between imperial and metric measurements, see pages 23–4.

Part One
Measuring Rules

1
The most important figure

The most important figure is that of the person who is going to wear the garment.

Before you can think about anything else, you must know how big the garment has to be. That is not the same as knowing the person's measurements. People like to wear clothes in different ways. When you are designing for a particular person, you can fit to his or her preferences, rather than using a standard shape. Find a garment that fits the person and take all the measurements from that. If you cannot do this, you will have to make an educated guess at the necessary measurements.

A good tape measure is essential. It must be flexible for measuring bodies, but a metal one will usually do for measuring garments. Over a long period of time, some tape measures stretch and become inaccurate. That would not matter if you were to take new measurements for every garment, but most people work partly to measurements they remember from previous occasions.

So how do you know if your tape measure has stretched? A metre stick or rule is a useful tool. It cannot stretch (although they do sometimes warp) so it can be used for checking the accuracy of your tape. It can also be used for taking measurements from a garment which has been laid flat. Metre rules are a bit long and unwieldy, however, especially if you are working in a restricted space. A metre is about four inches longer than a yard, so an old-fashioned yardstick will do the job just as well, but will not be marked in centimetres. You can work either in centimetres or inches. Most metre rules and tape measures come marked with both metric and imperial measurements, so you can convert from one to the other by comparing the measurements on your tape or rule. Many shorter rules no longer have inches on them. A standard 30cm ruler is too short for most garments, but a ruler of around 50 or 60cm is useful. You may find one in an art shop.

A basic calculator is essential to help you work out all the other figures.

2
Measuring a jumper

Jumpers, cardigans and jackets are the most commonly made garments. Once you know how to calculate the sizes for these, you should be able to apply the techniques to more unusual shapes. The arrowed lines on the following diagrams show the measurements you will need.

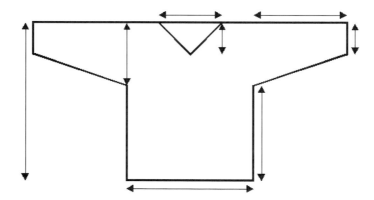

To find the measurements for a jumper, cardigan or jacket, take a garment of the right size, fasten any buttons and lay it flat. If the shape is being pulled in by any bands or fastenings, you should stretch it out as you take the measurements. You will certainly need to know all the dimensions shown in the diagrams, and there may be others.

A basic jumper opens up to give these pieces.

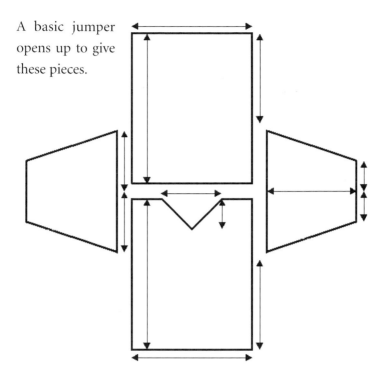

These measurements are only your starting point. They are the nearest thing you have to what you really want, but it is probably still not exactly right. You do not have to be content with the 'average' shape and dimensions given by commercial patterns.

It seems fairly obvious that, if you are tall, you should make your pattern longer and if you are small, you can shorten the pattern, but you need not stop there. Create the exact shape you want for your figure.

For a large middle, for example, a jumper is more flattering if it does not have to stretch tightly to fit. Making everything wider would make the shoulders too big, so change just the parts that need changing. Decide where it would need to be bigger, and by how much, and build this into your plan. It will probably mean adding a gentle slope to the sides of your garment.

A person with very wide shoulders and a narrow body would need the slope to go the opposite way, tapering in towards the lower edge. Again, start from the measurements you know are correct and work from there.

What was that about an opened up jumper?

3
Tense about tension?

In Britain knitters make a tension square to find their tension. In the United States they knit a swatch to calculate gauge. We are all doing the same thing.

Before you can do most of the other calculations you need, you have to know the tension (gauge) of your knitting. This varies from one yarn to another. You can discover your tension by knitting a sample piece first. Some knitters skip this step because it seems to be a waste of time to knit something that will not be used. Being sure of the size you are knitting will save you time in the long run. You may be able to begin with a piece that will not show afterwards, such as the inside of a pocket, and use that as the tension square. Some people recommend knitting a matching hat first (because it is small and quick) and using that to check the tension.

The sample must be knitted in the exact yarn and stitch of the garment, using the same needles. If you change anything, the tension could change.

The reason for knitting the sample is to find out how many stitches and rows you need to make one centimetre (or inch) of the knitting. Examples to show you how to calculate in both centimetres and inches are given on the following pages.

Many commercial patterns recommend measuring a square of 10cm (4in). It does not really matter what size it is if you know what you are doing and why you are doing it. The bigger your sample is, the more accurate your calculations will be. Do not try to measure just one centimetre (or one inch). A tiny mistake will become an enormous one by the time it is multiplied all over your garment.

Knit your sample piece and do to it everything you will do to the finished garment. If it has to be ironed, iron it. If the garment needs to be stretched out, sprayed and left to dry, then so does the sample. Some yarns even need to be washed before they reach their final shape.

When the sample is ready measure it very carefully. A piece of stocking stitch without any edging can be difficult to keep flat. You may have to resort to pinning it, so take care not to stretch it. I use a very thickly padded, firm board for jobs like this (*see* the Appendix on page 92 for instructions on how to make one). Use the pins to spear the knitting to the board, putting them in at an angle of about 45°. If you have no board, this will work equally well on a carpet.

It is not easy just to lay a tape measure on the knitting and count the stitches or rows, so put a pin at each end of the length you want to count and count the stitches or rows between the pins. Alternatively, use a piece of card with a 10cm (4in) square hole in it and count the stitches or rows you can see through the hole. The card must be cut accurately, but once you have made it you can keep it for use on every project. Eventually you will need to count the stitches in complex patterns, but you will find this easier once you have mastered the art of counting the basic stitches such as stocking or garter stitch.

Remember to make a note of your results. You will need this information later.

Counting garter stitch

Garter stitch (every row knit) is the easiest to count. It makes distinct ridges and each ridge is made up of two rows. You must be clear about the difference between the ridges and the rows and decide which you are going to use for your calculations. You can use either, but you must be consistent.

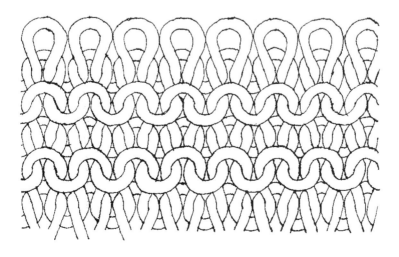

To find the number of stitches, count across the row. You will see that there are two sets of interlocking loops. Count either the top set or the bottom, but not both.

Counting stocking stitch

Stocking stitch is the most commonly used stitch. It consists of alternate rows of knit and purl, when you are working on two needles. If you work 'in the round', on a circular needle or a set of double pointed needles, you get the same effect by knitting every row.

The following examples show the front of stocking stitch, full size. Count the stitches and rows for yourself and you will soon discover exactly where to count. The two parts of the V make one stitch.

If you find it difficult to count on the front of the work, try turning it over. The back of stocking stitch gives small ridges, which some people prefer to count. There are the same number of ridges on the back as there are rows of Vs on the front.

Most people do not knit perfectly regular stitches all the time. These examples are therefore slightly uneven. Measuring across several centimetres or inches averages out the unevenness. If you have a larger piece of knitting, count the number of stitches in, say, 15cm (6in) and when you do the calculations divide by 15 (or 6) to find how many stitches make one centimetre (or inch).

Note

The examples show that you do not always get exactly the same number of stitches in 10cm as you do in 4in, so decide before you begin whether you are going to work in centimetres or inches, then make all your calculations in the same units.

Stitch tension: Example 1

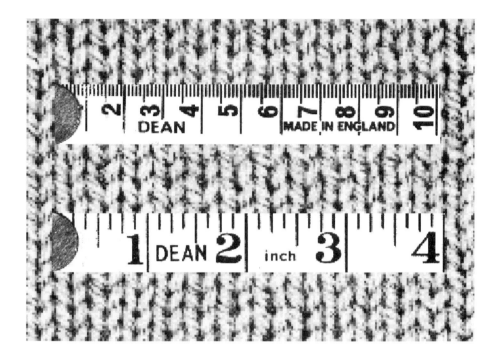

Centimetres

12 stitches make 10cm.

On average, each centimetre has (12 ÷ 10) stitches.

The stitch tension is 1.2 stitches to 1cm.

Inches

12 stitches make 4in.

On average, each inch has (12 ÷ 4) stitches.

The stitch tension is 3 stitches to 1in.

How to use your stitch tension: Example 1

These examples show you how to work out the number of stitches needed for the back of an average adult's jumper and a smaller, child-sized garment.

Stitch tension in centimetres

The sample has a stitch tension of 1.2 stitches to 1cm.

To make the back of a sweater 56cm wide:

You need 1.2 stitches for each centimetre, so you need 56 lots of 1.2, which is 67.2 stitches. Make 67.

To make a child's sweater 35cm wide:

You need 35 lots of 1.2, which makes 42.

Stitch tension in inches

To make a piece 22in wide:

At a tension of 3 stitches to 1in, you need 22 lots of 3, which is 66 stitches.

To make a 14in child's sweater, you need 14 lots of 3 stitches, which is 42.

Row tension: Example 1

Centimetres

18 rows make 10cm. On average, each centimetre has (18 ÷ 10) rows. The row tension is 1.8 rows to 1cm.

Inches

18 rows make 4in. On average, each inch has (18 ÷ 4) rows. The row tension is 4.5 rows to 1in.

How to use your row tension: Example 1

These examples show you how to work out the number of rows needed for a particular length of knitting, using the tension shown in the sample on page 15. Adjust the length for the size of garment you are making.

Row tension in centimetres

The sample shown has a row tension of 1.8 rows to a centimetre. You must knit 1.8 rows to make each centimetre of knitting.

To make a length of 30cm:

Using a tension of 1.8 rows to each centimetre, you need 30 lots of 1.8, which is 54 rows.

Row tension in inches

The sample shows a row tension of 4.5 rows to an inch. You must knit 4.5 rows to make every inch of knitting.

To make a length of 12in:

Using a tension of 4.5 rows to an inch, you must knit 12 lots of 4.5, which is 54 rows.

Stitch tension: Example 2

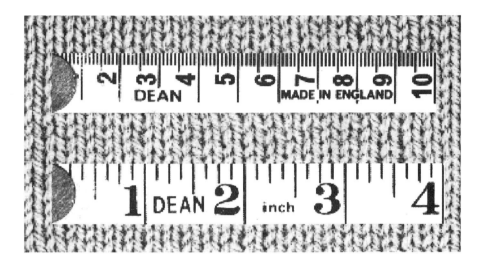

Centimetres

19 stitches make 10cm.

On average, each centimetre has (19 ÷ 10) stitches.

The stitch tension is 1.9 stitches to 1cm.

Inches

19.5 stitches make 4in.

On average, each inch has (19.5 ÷ 4) stitches.

The stitch tension is 4.875 stitches to 1in.

How to use your stitch tension: Example 2

The numbers in these examples are more difficult, but that is not a problem when you use a calculator.

Stitch tension in centimetres

For a 56cm back at a tension of 1.9 stitches per centimetre, you need 106.4 stitches (56 x 1.9), so make 106.

For a 35cm piece, you need 66.5 (35 x 1.9). You cannot make half a stitch, so make 66 or 67.

Stitch tension in inches

For a sweater 22in wide, you will need 22 times 4.875, which is 107.25 stitches. You cannot make a quarter of a stitch, so make 107.

For the child's 14in sweater, you would need 14 x 4.875. This comes to 68.25, so make 68.

Note

There is a slight difference between the answers for the centimetres and the inches. This is caused by rounding to the nearest half stitch when counting the stitches, and to the nearest whole centimetre when measuring.

Row tension: Example 2

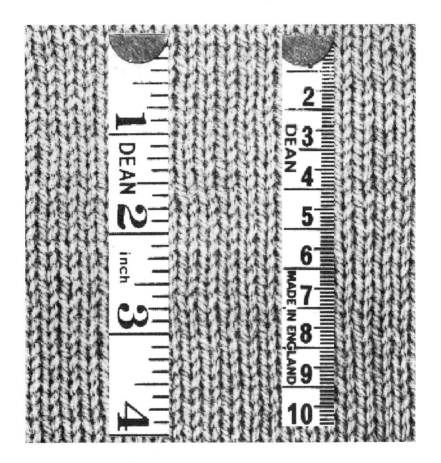

Centimetres

30 rows make 10cm. On average, each centimetre has (30 ÷ 10) rows. The row tension is 3 rows to 1cm.

Inches

31 rows make 4in. On average, each inch has (31 ÷ 4) rows. The row tension is 7.75 rows to 1in.

How to use your row tension: Example 2

Row tension in centimetres

At a tension of 3 rows to 1cm, you need 90 rows (3 x 30) to make a piece 30cm long.

Row tension in inches

Using 7.75 rows to the inch, you need 93 rows (7.75 x 12) to make a piece 12in long.

At-tension

By using the tension you have worked out you can now calculate the number of rows and stitches needed for any piece of knitting you want to make.

Use stitch tension when you are doing calculations involving the width of a piece of knitting. Use row tension for calculations about the length of the knitting.

Width and length refer to the piece of knitting when it is on the needles. This is not always the same direction as the length and width of the finished garment. If you knit a jumper sideways, for example, the number of stitches on the needle (width) decides how long the jumper will be, not how wide it will be. Make sure you know in which direction you are going for each piece.

4
Old and new measures

There is a lot of confusion about the sizing of knitting needles and balls of yarn. There are still many books and patterns around which use the old system of numbering, and this is what many people have grown up with. Modern British patterns give metric needle sizes (measured in millimetres) and metric amounts of yarn (measured in grams). Older patterns will have the old UK needle sizes and yarn measured in ounces. The USA has a completely different system of numbering needles.

Converting ounces to grams

One ounce is the same as 28.35g. The following chart shows how to change an old pattern from ounces to grams, to the nearest gram.

Ounces	Grams	Ounces	Grams
1	28	7	198
2	57	8	227
3	85	9	255
4	113	10	283
5	142	20	567
6	170	30	851

Example

To convert 16oz to grams: add the number of grams for 10 and 6oz.

$$283 + 170 = 453g$$

Needle sizes

This chart shows the comparative sizes of needles used in various parts of the world. It begins with the largest sizes. For some sizes there are no equivalents.

Metric (mm)	UK (old)	US
10	000	15
9	00	13
8	0	11
7½	1	
7	2	
6½	3	10½
6	4	10
5½	5	9
5	6	8
4½	7	7
		6
4	8	
3¾	9	5
3½		4
3	10	3
3	11	
2¾	12	2
2½		
2¼	13	1
2	14	0

Converting centimetres to inches

It is best to decide which units to use – either metric or imperial – and then make all your calculations using those units. You can avoid the need to convert anything.

This table shows the number of inches to the nearest quarter inch.

cm	in	cm	in
1	½	20	7¾
2	¾	30	11¾
3	1¼	40	15¾
4	1½	50	19¾
5	2	60	23½
6	2½	70	27½
7	2¾	80	31½
8	3¼	90	35½
9	3½	100	39¼
10	4		

Example

To change 143cm to inches: look at the table to find the number of inches for 100cm and for 40cm and 3cm, and add them together.

$$39¼ + 15¾ + 1¼ = 56¼in$$

Converting inches to centimetres

Inches are bigger than centimetres, so there will always be fewer inches than centimetres. This table shows the number of centimetres to the nearest half centimetre.

in	cm	cm	in
1	2.5	20	51.0
2	5.0	30	76.0
3	7.5	40	101.5
4	10.0	50	127.0
5	12.5	60	152.5
6	15.0	70	178.0
7	18.0	80	203.0
8	20.5	90	228.5
9	23.0	100	254.0
10	25.0		

Example

To change 68 inches into centimetres: use the table to find how many centimetres make 60in and how many make 8in, then add them together.

$$152.5 + 20.5 = 173cm$$

5
Calculating the amount of yarn

The only reliable way to find out how much yarn you will need is to knit a piece of the garment to see how far one ball goes, then work your calculations from that.

Manufacturers are now putting lengths on balls of yarn. This is more useful than knowing the weight in a ball, because the amount of yarn in two balls of the same weight can vary enormously, depending on the content and, sometimes, the colour. Knowing the length is helpful if you want to compare with something you have made before. If there is a shorter length in the ball, you will need more balls to finish a garment. A lightweight yarn could have a longer length, so you would need fewer balls.

Assuming you have nothing else to compare with, knit up one ball of your chosen yarn and work out the area it covers. You must calculate the areas, not just the lengths of the pieces. Measurements only work in one direction. Measuring in two directions automatically gives you a two-dimensional shape. As soon as you start covering a surface you should be thinking about area.

Try to make the piece you are measuring representative of the whole garment. Ribs and heavily textured patterns use up more yarn than something like stocking stitch, so if your garment is mainly plain, do not work out the yarn based on a ribbed sample. To make life easy, your sample, which can be part of one of the pieces of your real garment, should be a rectangle. To find the area of a rectangle, multiply the distance in one direction by the distance in the other direction. Work in either centimetres or inches, but use the same for everything. Your answer will be in square centimetres or square inches.

Example

One ball of yarn knits a piece 40cm by 25cm.
The area is 40 x 25 = 1,000 sq cm.

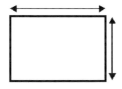

The jumper has two pieces which each measure 50cm by 60cm, and two sleeves which measure 46cm by 40cm.

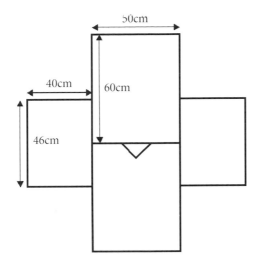

Area of back: 50 x 60 = 3,000
Area of front: 50 x 60 = 3,000

Area of first sleeve: 46 x 40 = 1,840
Area of second sleeve: 46 x 40 = 1,840
Total area: 3,000 + 3,000 + 1,840 + 1,840 = 9,680 sq cm

From the calculation opposite, each ball of yarn will make 1,000 sq cm, so divide the total area by this number to find out how many balls you need:
9,680 ÷ 1,000 = 9.68.

You would need at least 10 balls. Allow more for the parts that use more yarn, such as ribs. The front needs slightly less than the back because of the neckline, but this is not enough to make a significant difference. It is better to overestimate and buy too much yarn rather than not have enough.

Areas of complex shapes

When working out the amount of yarn it can only ever be an estimate. This is why commercial patterns seem to get it wrong so often. They always try to ensure that you have more than enough. Work on the same principles. Do not try to be too accurate. Make things easy for yourself by working out approximate areas in the way you best understand – then allow a bit extra.

You could estimate the area of a sleeve, for example, by finding the area of the rectangle into which it would fit. That would give you a bigger area than you actually need, so you may want to calculate more accurately.

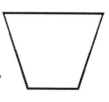

You could split the shape up into bits that you do know how to calculate. You do not need any complicated mathematical rules. Use what you know already – and common sense.

Here is the sleeve split into a rectangle and two triangles.

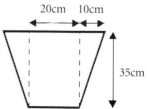

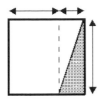

Imagine turning over one of the triangles and moving it to the other side. There would now be two rectangles.

Area of larger rectangle: 20 x 35 = 700
Area of smaller rectangle: 10 x 35 = 350
Total area: 700 + 350 = 1,050 sq cm

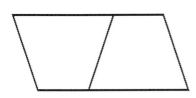

Another way to work out the area of the sleeves is to imagine the two sleeves fitted together and work out the area as one piece.

It looks like a difficult shape, but if you imagine chopping a triangle off one end . . .

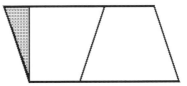

. . . and putting it at the other end . . .

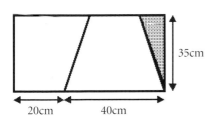

35cm

. . . it becomes a simple rectangle, with a length which is the total of the top and bottom edges of the sleeve.

20cm   40cm

Area: 35 x (40 + 20) = 2,100 sq cm

This is the area of both sleeves together, so it is double the answer found before.

Most garment pieces go in pairs and it is often easier to calculate the area by mentally joining them together first.

It is almost impossible to work out exactly the amount of yarn you will need. An estimate is an educated guess. If possible get more than you think you need.

Part Two
Calculating Rules

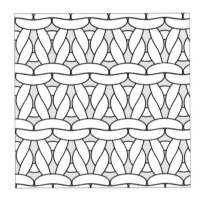

6
Back and front

When you have finished your measuring and worked out your basic tension and overall size, you will need to start considering some parts of your garment in more detail.

Most simple sweaters and jackets have a basic rectangular shape for the back and front. The back does not usually need any shaping at all. The front will need to be split in two for a jacket, and will probably need neck shaping for any garment. It is easiest to start with the rectangle for the back.

Back

Use the measurements you got from your favourite jumper (pages 6–7), and the tension from your sample (pages 9–11), to work out how many stitches you need for the back, and how many rows you will have to knit to complete the rectangle.

Edgings

If you are used to commercial knitting patterns you will probably expect to start with some sort of rib or edging. I prefer to add these pieces later, usually by picking up stitches and knitting in a new direction. The major disadvantage of adding them later is that your work will probably roll because it has nothing to stop it. The great advantages are that the shape of the knitting is not distorted by being pulled in by a tighter band,

and you can also make any minor alterations to the length, width or style at the last minute.

The tension for the edging might be different from the main pieces. You should work another sample to calculate the tension for this part. If you prefer to rely on the very un-mathematical method of guesswork, adding the bands last means that you only have a little bit to undo if it goes wrong.

Some types of edging are briefly mentioned here, for those who cannot start without them, and you will find more information later in Picking up Stitches (pages 70–4).

A rib worked on the same number of stitches always pulls the work inwards. If you want the rib to be very tight, you can begin with fewer stitches than the main part and increase later.

A folded hem, in the same stitch, will be at the same tension as the rest of the garment. To make it lie flat, the folded-in part needs to be a tiny bit smaller than the outside. You can achieve this by using smaller needles or having fewer stitches.

Garter stitch and moss stitch give a good, firm edging but spread the work, so you need at least 10% fewer stitches, unless you want the edges to flare out.

When you have worked your edging, make sure you have the right number of stitches for the main part of the rectangle. Remember to take account of the length of the edging. It adds to the length you knit for the main part.

Front

The front, or fronts, will need to match the back. Make sure they match by counting the number of rows, not by measuring. Most knitting stretches as you are doing it and will relax again afterwards. Narrow pieces stretch downwards more than wide ones.

For each front of a jacket, you need at least half the number of stitches used for the back. You may want to add extra if you are working the front edging at the same time, and you will need one extra if you intend to stitch on an edging, or pick up any stitches.

Shaped backs and fronts

The majority of people are quite happy with the basic rectangular shape, but it is not suitable for everyone.

If the jumper needs to be narrow at the hips and wide at the chest, you can take account of this. Decide on the measurements for the narrowest part, the widest part, and the distance between the two.

Start with the stitches for the narrow measurement and gradually increase to the number for the wider measurement. Use your row tension to change the distance between them into a number of rows. The increases will go in pairs, one at each end of a row, and should be spread evenly in the number of rows.

For a person who is wider at the waist than at the chest, the jumper will fit better if you start by making it big enough to go round the waist and then decrease towards the chest. Again you will need the narrowest and widest measurements, converted into stitches, and the distance between them, converted into rows.

Start with the larger number and make evenly spaced decreases at the ends of rows enough times to get down to the number you need for the chest.

Example

The sweater which Kangarule is holding on page 4 is this shape:

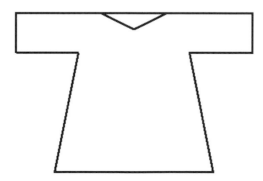

The sweater has to be wider round the waist than round the chest.

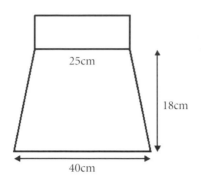

Measure the widest part, the narrowest part, and how far up the narrowest part should be. The diagram shows the back with some sample measurements.

Remember that this is not for a human shape.

At a tension of 2 stitches and 3 rows to a centimetre, this would need 80 stitches at the bottom, but only 50 at the level of the armholes.

It would need 54 rows to get to the armholes. In these 54 rows, 30 stitches need to disappear. The two sides should be even, so 15 pairs of decreases will be needed.

If you decrease on every third row, you would use up 45 of the rows, which is not quite enough. If you decrease on every fourth row, you would need 60 rows to make all the decreases. A mixture of the two would be about right. Decrease on the fourth row, and the following third, then fourth, then third, until you have 60 stitches left.

If you need much more room at the front than at the back, you do not have to have them the same width. The parts where they come together must match, however. The side seams should be the same, or one part will hang down more than the other. The shoulders must also match. A few extra stitches can be taken into the neck shaping if there is nowhere else for them to go.

7
Sleeve shaping

The easiest sleeve to knit is a rectangle with no shaping at all. This shape will easily join to a drop-shoulder style garment, or it can be slightly set into a square armhole. These two alternatives are shown on opposite sides of the diagram below.

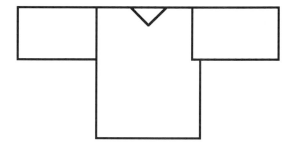

The rectangle can be knitted in any direction as long as it is the right size to become the sleeve. The problem of finishing the lower edge of the sleeve can be left until later. It may not even need finishing. It could be left to hang straight, or it could have some kind of turn-back cuff. It could also be pulled in by adding a tighter cuff, to alter the appearance completely.

Most sleeves are not rectangular. They usually slope gently from the cuff to the top. The slope can be steep or gentle, depending on the effect required. Two examples are shown on this sweater.

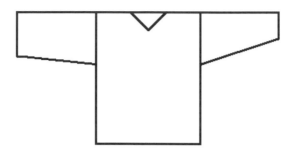

You do not have to start at the bottom and work upwards. It is the final shape that is important.

Start at either end. The shape will be exactly the same.

The following instructions explain how to shape this type of sleeve.

Simple sleeve calculations

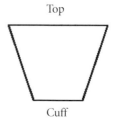

The instructions are very similar whether you go from top to bottom, or from bottom to top. My example starts from the cuff.

1 Decide the width of the top of the sleeve and the width of the bottom before any cuff is added to pull it in.

2 From your stitch tension, work out how many stitches are needed at each end.

3 Subtract the small number from the large number. The answer tells you how many extra stitches you need by the time you reach the top of the sleeve.

4 Divide the number by 2, because the increased stitches always go in pairs – one at each side of the sleeve.

5 Decide the length of the sleeve, not counting the cuff.

6 From your row tension, work out how many rows are needed to make this length.

7 Divide the number of rows (above) by the number of increases you found in no. 4. Ignore any decimals in your answer.

8 If the answer is 4, increase both ends of every fourth row. If the answer is 5, increase every fifth row, etc.

Example

This example is the main part of a sleeve with a tension of 1.2 stitches and 1.8 rows to 1cm.

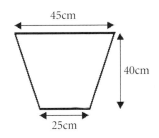

The lower edge of the sleeve needs 30 stitches (25 x 1.2) and the top edge needs 54 stitches (45 x 1.2). The whole sleeve needs 72 rows (40 x 1.8).

You must increase 24 stitches (54 – 30) evenly up the sleeve. The increases go in pairs, so you need 12 of them. This divides into the 72 rows 6 times. Increase on every sixth row.

When the answers work out exactly, as in the example, that means the last increase will be on your last row of working. This is not a good idea, because it is very close to the top of the sleeve and may become part of a seam or other shaping. Avoid this by moving all the increases down a couple of rows, but still keeping the correct spacing. In the above example, therefore, you could increase on rows 3, 9, 15, 21, etc.

Whenever you knit a sleeve, work the number of increases you calculated in no. 4 of the method given on the previous page. You may find this does not give enough rows for the length you wanted, because of the rounding errors in your calculations. The last few rows at the top of the sleeve can be straight until you have done the number of rows you found in no. 5.

This straight section will not be noticed on your sleeve. It could be more of a problem if you decide to work the sleeve from the top downwards, by decreasing from the larger measurement to the smaller. The extra rows will be at the bottom end of the sleeve. If the sleeve is to have a cuff, these rows certainly will not be noticed. If the shaping is more obvious, you will need to use the more accurate, but more complex, calculations which follow.

Note

I usually prefer to work sleeves from the top downwards, as adjustments can be made to the length at every stage.

Simultaneous equations

Using the rules for Sleeve Calculations on page 39, this sleeve needs 16 increases. They should occur every 3 rows. It would take 48 rows to complete the shaping, and 12 straight rows to finish the sleeve.

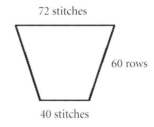

72 stitches

60 rows

40 stitches

To spread the shaping more evenly, the calculations need to be more accurate.

Dividing the 60 rows by the 16 increases gives an answer of 3.75. Because this is between 3 and 4, alternating increases after 3 then 4 rows would be a better fit.

Instead of 16 lots of 3, this would give 8 lots of 7, which is 56, and would leave 4 rows, which would make a short, straight piece at the top of the sleeve.

You could decide to work the 7 fourth row increases first, followed by the 7 third row increases, to change the look of the sleeve slightly.

Sometimes it is even more difficult to work out the numbers and simultaneous equations should be used.

Simultaneous just means that things happen at the same time. Simultaneous equations are two rules that must both work at once. The two things that must happen here are that the decreases must come to the total you need and the spacing of the decreases must fill (or almost fill) the number of rows you have available. Using letters for the missing numbers helps to make this clearer.

When you divide the number of rows by the number of increases, you are almost certain to get an answer with decimals in it. The whole numbers either side of that number tell you what size spaces you need between the increases. For instance, if you get an answer of 3.146, you will need some third row increases and some fourth row increases. You do not know how many of each you need, so call them x and y. When they are added together, they must give the total number of increases.

$$x + y = \text{increases}$$

The total number of rows must be some mixture of x lots of one of your increases added to y lots of your other increases.

x times your first increase spacing + y times your second increase spacing = number of rows

There will only be one value for x and y that will make both of these rules work at the same time. If you are not sure about how to work out simultaneous equations, the easiest thing is to try different values for x and y. You know what their total is, so there is a limited range of possible answers.

Example

In this example there must be 20 pairs of increases. Dividing 94 by 20 gives an answer of 4.7, so the increases can be at intervals of 4 or 5 rows.

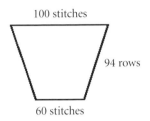

100 stitches

94 rows

60 stitches

To find out how many of each type there should be: x can stand for the number of fourth row increases and y can stand for the number of fifth row increases. There are 20 increases altogether, so x added to y must be 20. There are x lots of 4 rows and y lots of 5 rows.

$$x + y = 20$$
$$4x + 5y = 94$$

The only answer that will work for both is x = 6, y = 14, so it needs 6 fourth row increases and 14 fifth row increases if the increases are to go to the very top.

Most commercial patterns only have increases on even numbered rows. If you want to do the same, you must increase on fourth and sixth rows. The equations become:

$$x + y = 20$$
$$4x + 6y = 94$$

The only answer that will work for both is x = 13, y = 7, so you will need to increase on every fourth row 13 times, and on every sixth row 7 times.

8
Sleeve tops

Raglans

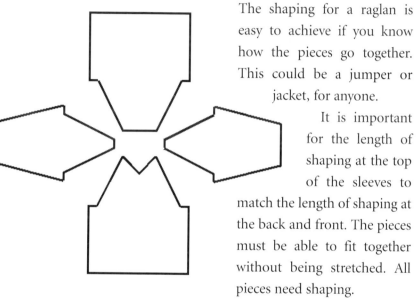

The shaping for a raglan is easy to achieve if you know how the pieces go together. This could be a jumper or jacket, for anyone.

It is important for the length of shaping at the top of the sleeves to match the length of shaping at the back and front. The pieces must be able to fit together without being stretched. All pieces need shaping.

The bottom part of the sleeve can be shaped according to the same rules as for any other sleeve. The lower parts of the

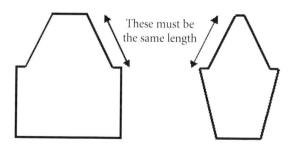

These must be the same length

back and front of the garment can also be any shape you want. Raglans are not usually as baggy as drop-shoulder styles, but they can be. It is a matter of personal preference. It is the shaping for the top of the garment that is important here.

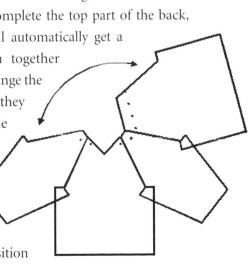

The shaping for the top of the sleeve begins with a few cast-off stitches. The stitches cast off on the back will join those cast off on the sleeve, so there must be the same number of each. The same applies at the front.

The top of a raglan sleeve usually narrows to a very small number of stitches at the neck edge. If a larger neck opening is required, more stitches can be left at this edge. If the hole is to be larger all round, do not complete the top part of the back, front or sleeves, and you will automatically get a larger hole where they join together lower down. This does not change the shape of the pieces, or the way they join together. It is not possible to show this in a completely flattened out view.

The arrow shows where the second sleeve would join to the back, and the dotted line shows the position of a possible wider neckline.

A raglan can have a close-fitting neckline or almost any other style you want. The shaping for the neck usually goes on within the sloping edges of the raglan, as shown below. The neck shaping will not interfere with the raglan shaping, although you may need to be thinking about them both at once.

The back and sleeves would be the same for any of these. The slope of the back would match that of the front.

Raglan calculations

Start by working out the slope for the back.

You need to know how many rows should be worked between the start of the armhole and the neck edge, and how many stitches should be left by the time you get to the neck.

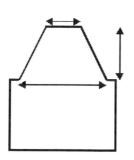

Work these out by measuring and using your tension square, as before (*see* pages 10–11).

When you do the calculations, remember that a few stitches are cast off at each side at the beginning of the shaping. This is to make the sleeve fit more comfortably under the arm. The width of these cast-off stitches should be between 2 and 3cm. Allow more stitches for a large person than you would for a smaller person.

The general principles are the same as for other sleeve shaping, except that, if you are working from the bottom of the sleeve upwards, all the shaping will now be decreasing not increasing. Many commercial patterns are arranged so that the numbers always work out simply. When you are designing your own garments, it is not always so easy. You will have to use simultaneous equations to solve the problem.

Example

The full width of this back is 120 stitches. 5 are to be cast off on each of the first two shaping rows, leaving 110, so 80 stitches will need to be decreased in the remaining 70 rows. This is 40 pairs of decreases.

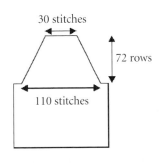

30 stitches

72 rows

110 stitches

70 divided by 40 is 1.75. Taking the whole number either side of this, there must be some decreases on every row and some on every second row. Call them x and y.

$$x + y = 40 \ (total \ decreases)$$
$$1x + 2y = 70 \ (rows)$$

The only solution that works for both is when x = 10 and y = 30. Decrease on every row 10 times and on alternate rows 30 times.

The top of the sleeve and the top of the back (and front) have to be the same length so that they can fit together. You must have the same number of rows on each. You may be lucky enough to be able to use the same combination of decreases on the sleeve as you worked out for the back, or you may be able to alter the

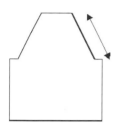
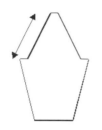

width of the sleeve a little to make that combination fit. If you do not want to do that, you can make another pair of simultaneous equations for the sleeve, and slope them in the same way.

Semi-fitted sleeves

On more tailored garments the sleeve top can be fitted more closely to the body. The armhole is not as deep as it is on most other styles.

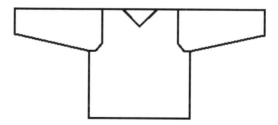

A semi-fitted sleeve looks like this. Under the arm it has a straight piece on both the sleeve and body, where a few stitches have been cast off. This is followed by a slope on both and a flat top to the sleeve, with no further shaping on the body.

Measure the distance across the back at the shoulders, to where you want the sleeves to be, and work out how many stitches need to be left at this point. Find the difference between the number of stitches at the widest point of the back and the number across the shoulders, and divide the answer in two. That is the number of stitches that need to be removed at each side by casting off and making the slope. The slope is usually worked by decreasing on alternate rows. After you have cast off the first few stitches (about 2.5cm wide) decrease until all the stitches you do not want have gone. Knit the rest of the body straight. Shape the sleeves in exactly the same way, casting off all remaining stitches loosely when the shaping is complete.

The finished sleeve will look like this, although the corners will be smoothed into curves as the pieces are joined together.

Example

The back has 120 stitches and needs 84 across the shoulders. Cast off enough stitches for 2–3cm at each side. In this example that would be six at each side and there would be 108 stitches left. Decrease one stitch at each end of every right-side row until there are 84 stitches left. Continue straight.

At the top of the sleeve, cast off the same number of stitches and make the same number of decreases, then cast off all the stitches that are left.

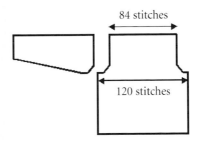

84 stitches

120 stitches

Set-in sleeves

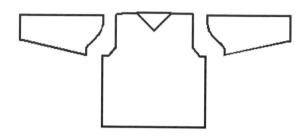

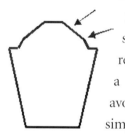

Some designs call for sleeves to be even more closely fitted. This is achieved by shaping the top of the sleeve so that it follows the curves of the body and results in a sleeve with a much rounder top. This is a more complicated shape and is probably best avoided until you are more experienced at getting the simpler shapes right.

9
Neck openings

You can have the exact neckline you want, by careful measuring and counting. You do not have to rely on the instructions in commercial patterns.

You need to know the width and depth of your neckline and the row and stitch tensions. The example will be in centimetres, but the method is the same in any units.

Example: V-neck

Suppose you want to make a V-neck which is 15cm wide and 15cm deep, and you are working at a tension of 2.1 stitches and 3 rows to a centimetre. The neckline 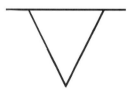 *will be 32 stitches wide (15 x 2.1) and 45 rows deep (15 x 3).*

Because the neck is symmetrical, half the stitches will be at each side so there will be 16 stitches to be decreased in the space of 45 rows.

You could decrease every third row, so that by the time you reach the top you have only decreased 15 stitches, not 16. This would make little difference to the overall design, provided that other pieces will still fit to it.

To make the shaping fit exactly, you will need two stages of decreasing and will have to use simultaneous equations again. The solution for the above example is to decrease on every second row three times and on every third row 13 times.

The average width for the back neck of a round, crew or polo neck is roughly one-third of the width of the back of the garment. For babies and small children this will not give an opening large enough for the head to go through. Babies' heads are not in the same proportion to their bodies as adults' heads are. Make the neckline bigger by incorporating some sort of opening. This also applies for anyone with restricted movement who may have trouble taking the garment on and off.

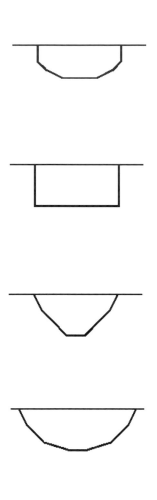

Any curved neckline is really made up from a series of straight sections. Break down the curve into its various sections and it becomes easy to work out.

Where the slope is completely flat, you should cast off some stitches. Where it is nearly flat, you need to decrease often. As it gets steeper, the decreases are less frequent. Measure, count and calculate each piece of the curve separately.

Example: curved neck

This neck has three sections to calculate: the flat bottom and two slightly sloping sections at each side. For each section you need to know the number of rows and stitches.

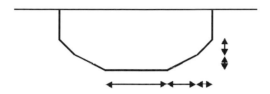

The neck is to be 24 rows deep. If the overall width of the neck is 34 stitches and the flat part at the front is 12, that leaves 22 for the rest of the shaping, which would be 11 from each side. About half of these can be incorporated into the first slope, so decrease at each end of every row for six rows. Now five more have to go, in a gentler slope, so decrease on the next five alternate rows. This uses up 16 rows (6 + 10), so you need to knit 8 more.

The exact shape you get will vary according to the stitch you are using. The thickness of the yarn does not change the shape; it only changes the size. The slope produced when you decrease on every row will be almost the same for any type of yarn, in a particular stitch. You may need more, or fewer, decreases when you use a different yarn, because the whole garment uses more, or fewer, stitches and any shaping stays in proportion.

If the slope produced when you decrease on every row is not flat enough, you will have to decrease more stitches on the first few rows at the beginning of the neck shaping. Cast off two, three, or more stitches at the neck edge for a few rows.

An easy way to get the neck shaping right is to knit the back of the sweater first and then use it to work out what happens at the front. Draw the neckline you want on a piece of card, cut it out and place the cut-out on your knitting. Alternatively, mark the shape directly onto the knitting with pins or a fade-away pen. You will then be able to count how many stitches need to be decreased and from which rows they should be taken.

10
Curved edges

Curves occur most often at necklines, but any piece of knitting can be curved. It could be the bottom edge of a jacket, the end of a scarf, or a teddy bear's head.

Mathematically a curve is made up from a series of straight sections joined together. The shorter those straight pieces are, the smoother the curve will look. Long straight sections will be more obvious than a lot of little ones.

Knitting is very flexible and it is easy to make something look like a curve when it is really made up of straight edges. The way the curve is finished will disguise all the straight bits. Usually a curved piece and an unshaped piece will fit together and pull against each other into a smooth curve. For instance a neckline which is finished off with a few rows of straight knitting will look like a gentle curve, even when it was originally made from five or six straight sections.

Do not attempt to attach more than a couple of rows of straight knitting onto a curve (unless it is a very gentle curve), without including some shaping in the new piece. If the curve curls inwards, you will need to lose some stitches or it will not lie flat, because there will be too much knitting to fit inside the curve. If you are working round the outside of a curve going the other way, the new rows will not be able to stretch far enough to go round the curve and will make it wrinkle.

Where two shaped pieces come together, the angles will be exaggerated if the shapings meet at a point. Think about the effect of this and whether you would prefer to stagger the lines of shaping.

11
Pockets

Pockets should have openings large enough to get your hands in, be big enough to hold whatever you put in them, and be in a convenient place.

Before you add pockets to a garment, think seriously about whether you really need them. They often encourage people to put their hands in, and children in particular use them to twist and turn a garment in ways it was never meant to go. Pockets also get loaded with all sorts of weighty and lumpy items, and this can stretch and distort the knitted fabric.

Pocket sizes

If you must include pockets, do not make them any bigger than they need to be, to prevent them being filled up with unnecessary, heavy objects. The average pocket is slightly wider than the hand, so that the hand can slip in and out easily. The depth is usually slightly more than the width. Work out the width needed by measuring the flat hand. The opening should be big enough to get your hand in, but not big enough to let things fall out. Make sure the edging will not stretch excessively, as that would look messy and could allow things to fall out.

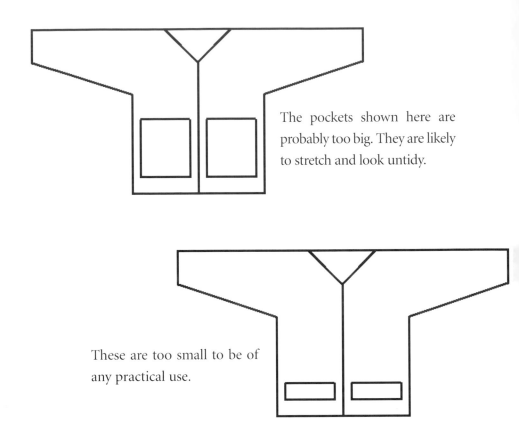

The pockets shown here are probably too big. They are likely to stretch and look untidy.

These are too small to be of any practical use.

Positioning pockets

The position of the pockets is also important. Do not put them where you cannot reach them easily. If they are too low you will have to bend over and stretch to get your hands to the bottom of them. If they are too high, or too far round the side, you will need to be a contortionist to get into them.

Decide on a convenient placing by putting your hands in a comfortable position and getting someone else to take the measurements. You will need to know how far away from the side seam the pockets should be, as well as the distance down from the shoulder. Do not measure the distance from the bottom of the sweater, unless you intend to re-measure every time you knit a different garment. A pocket 10cm from the bottom of an extra-long tunic would not be as convenient as one 10cm from the bottom of a normal-length jacket. Make sure you know whether the measurements are to the top, middle or bottom of the pocket, so that you can position it exactly where you want it.

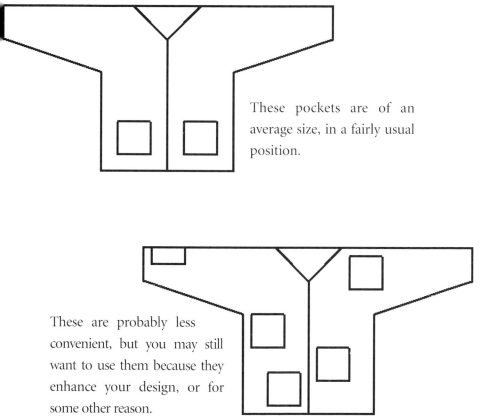

These pockets are of an average size, in a fairly usual position.

These are probably less convenient, but you may still want to use them because they enhance your design, or for some other reason.

Pocket styles

Horizontal openings

There are many different types of pocket. The simplest would be a rectangle stitched along three of its sides onto the outside of the garment. Use  your tension findings (*see* pages 10–11) to work out the size of the rectangle. This is easy, but might not be the most attractive pocket.

Another style which also uses a simple rectangle is for the extra piece to form a lining to the main pieces of the garment. Knit the rectangle first, but do not cast off at the end of it. Knit the main part of the garment up to the level of the top edge of the pocket. Work across to where the top of the pocket will be, then substitute the stitches of the rectangle for the same number of stitches on the main piece. The whole row should have the same number of stitches as it had before. Keep knitting on these stitches. The stitches from the main piece that are not being used can either be cast off, or finished with an edging later.

When a thick garment has a pocket like this, it can be very bulky. If this is a problem, the rectangle for the inside can be made of matching, but thinner yarn. You would need to make another tension square for this new yarn. The rectangle would almost certainly need fewer stitches than the number needed for the pocket in the main piece of the garment. When the stitches from the main piece are changed for the rectangle pieces, you will need to reduce the number of stitches on the rectangle until you have the right number. You do this by decreasing evenly across the row the number of stitches you need to lose. (There will be more about exactly how to do this later – *see* page 63.) Do not change the number of stitches on the main piece, or you will change the size of your garment.

Example

The width you need for the pocket top might be 20 stitches and the fine lining might be 30 stitches wide.

Where the lining joins to the main piece it will need to lose 10 stitches. You must decrease 10 times across the row. If you knit 1 and then knit 2 together all across, you will get the correct number.

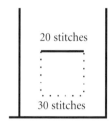

Vertical openings

Another easy pocket is one that fits into the side seams. The opening for this will be vertical, instead of horizontal as above.

When you stitch the side seam, leave a hole big enough for your hand. Make an extra piece to become the lining of the pocket. It can be any shape you want, except that one edge must match the edge of the

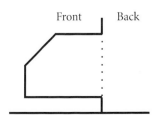

garment where it is to join. If the edge of the garment is straight, the edge of the pocket must also be straight. If the garment is shaped, the pocket should be the same shape. A rectangle is the easiest shape for the lining, but it may be better to adapt this. The edge of the pocket has to be stitched to the edge of the back of the garment. The other sides of the pocket then have to be stitched to the front of the garment. It is possible to stitch the pocket to the main piece of the garment so that it can hardly be seen, but changing its shape sometimes makes it blend into a pattern and become even less noticeable. The edge of the front will have a piece left that has nothing to join to and this may need some sort of finishing to make it neat.

A pocket may have a vertical opening, even when it is not set into a seam. Decide how far across the garment the opening should be and where the bottom edge should be. At this point, split the stitches into two sections (one for each side of the opening) and knit the two pieces separately until you reach the level of the top of the slit, then knit across all stitches so the main piece joins back into one piece with the same number of stitches that you had before. Finish the pocket in the same way as one joined into a seam.

There are many other pocket variations. They can be at other angles on the garment, in contrasting colours or of unusual shapes. When you have got used to positioning the simple ones correctly, you can try other possibilities.

12
Getting the stitches you want

The following rules work in the same way whether you are increasing or decreasing. Just remember whether you need to end up with more or less than you started with.

It is very easy to make 48 stitches change to 24. Knit two together across all 48 and you will have 24 stitches left.

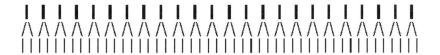

In the same way 24 stitches can become 48 by increasing after each one.

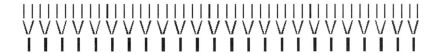

And 48 can easily become 36 because, for every four of the original stitches, you now need only three. Each four can become three by knitting two then knitting the next two together.

Any shaping usually looks better if it is centred, so you could move everything along one stitch, by knitting the first stitch without decreasing.

By changing the groups of three into fours, 36 become 48. Increase after every third stitch.

It is more difficult for 48 to become 30. The easy way is to decrease the stitches in the middle of the row, instead of doing it evenly all across. In some circumstances this would be a good solution. It still needs some thought to make sure the decreases are in the middle. If 18 stitches have to go, that means that the centre 36 have to be knitted together in twos. There will be 12 stitches unaccounted for, so six of these should be at each end of the row.

In the pattern below the 2s would disappear, leaving 30 1s.

1111111212121212121212121212121212121212111111

If it started as a row of 30 stitches needing to be increased to 48, add the 2s to the original stitches.

This method produces the correct number of stitches but all the shaping is in the middle of the row. That may be exactly what you want. For instance you might want your jacket to have a blouson effect in the middle of the back without too much extra fullness under the arms. On the other hand, you might not be happy with all the shaping at the bottom of your sleeve being on one side with nothing underneath.

There are several different ways of working out how and where to increase or decrease. The method you choose will depend on what you find easiest to understand and the effect you are trying to create.

Even spacing for shaping

When the increases or decreases have to be even the only sure way to get it right is with simultaneous equations.

Using the same example as above, 18 stitches have to be lost. Some of the decreases will need to be from blocks of 2 stitches and some will need to be from blocks of 3.

$$x + y = 18 \text{ (the number of decreases)}$$
$$2x + 3y = 48 \text{ (the number of stitches)}$$
The answers which work for both are $x = 6$ and $y = 12$

Decrease 6 times in blocks of 2 stitches (knit the 2 together) and decrease 12 times in blocks of 3 stitches (knit 1 and knit 2 together). The groups can be placed wherever you like across the row.

When the process is reversed and you need to increase from 30 to 48, you get an answer between 1 and 2 when you divide. The equations are:

$$x + y = 18$$
$$x + 2y = 30$$

These are also solved by $x = 6$ and $y = 12$. Increase every stitch 6 times and every second stitch 12 times.

Charts for increasing and decreasing

These charts show two more ways which may help you to work out your increases or decreases. They are alternatives to the previous methods and may help you to visualize what has to happen to your stitches.

You need to know the number of stitches before and after the increases or decreases.

Divide the smaller number by the larger and you will always get an answer of less than 1.

In the first column of the chart opposite, find the number nearest to your answer. The pattern on that line will show you the increases or decreases you need to make. Work all across your row using this pattern and you will get the number of stitches you wanted.

| means work normally
/\   means work 2 together/make 2 from stitch
/I\   means work 3 together/make 3 from stitch

.333	/|\										
.364	/\	/|\	/|\	/|\							
.375	/\	/|\	/|\								
.4	/\	/|\									
.417	/|\	/\	/|\	/\	/|\						
.428	/\	/\	/|\								
.444	/\	/\	/\	/|\							
.455	/\	/\	/\	/\	/|\						
.5	/\										
.545	|	/\	/\	/\	/\	/\					
.555	|	/\	/\	/\	/\						
.571	|	/\	/\	/\							
.583	|	/\	/\	|	/\	/\	/\				
.6	|	/\	/\								
.625	|	/\	|	/\	/\						
.636	|	/\	|	/\	|	/\	/\				
.666	|	/\									
.7	/\	|	/\	|	/\	|	|				
.714	/\	|	/\	|	|						
.727	/\	|	|	/\	|	|	/\	|			
.75	|	|	/\								
.777	/\	|	|	/\	|	|	|				
.8	|	|	/\								
.818	/\	|	|	|	/\	|	|	|	|		
.833	/\	|	|	|	|						
.857	/\	|	|	|	|	|					
.875	/\	|	|	|	|	|	|				
.888	/\	|	|	|	|	|	|	|			
.9	/\	|	|	|	|	|	|	|	|		
.909	/\	|	|	|	|	|	|	|	|	|	
.917	/\	|	|	|	|	|	|	|	|	|	|

In the second chart opposite, you will need to calculate the number of the first column in the same way as for the first chart. When you know the number, look at the rest of the line to see what groupings will fit your requirements exactly. The A column is the larger number, so if you are decreasing it tells you the groups you should look at for placing your decreases. The B column tells you where the increases should be.

This chart may help you to arrange your increases or decreases in a way that will help them blend into a design. It shows you different ways of achieving the same overall effect. For instance, decreasing groups of 12 stitches to make groups of 8 would have the same effect as decreasing groups of 9 to make groups of 6.

If you had a row of 36 stitches, it might have a 12-stitch repeat in the design. To keep the design looking the same right across you could decrease in the same positions in each of the three repeats of the pattern.

If your design has a 9-stitch repeat, you could decrease three stitches in the same positions in each of the four repeats.

This type of decreasing or increasing is very important if it is in a prominent position. The circular yoke of a sweater or jacket could look very busy and unbalanced if the decreases are not planned carefully.

	A	B	A	B	A	B	A	B	A	B	A	B
.333	12	4					9	3				
.364			11	4								
.375									8	3		
.4					10	4						
.417	12	5										
.428											7	3
.444							9	4				
.455			11	5								
.5	12	6			10	5			8	4		
.545			11	6								
.556							9	5				
.57											7	4
.583	12	7										
.6					10	6						
.625									8	5		
.636			11	7								
.666	12	8					9	6				
.7					10	7						
.714											7	5
.727			11	8								
.75	12	9							8	6		
.777							9	7				
.8					10	8						
.818			11	9								
.833	12	10										
.857											7	6
.875									8	7		
.888							9	8				
.9					10	9						
.909			11	10								
.917	12	11										

13
Picking up stitches

You often need to calculate the number of stitches to pick up along the edge of a piece of knitting. This could be to add a band knitted sideways, or any other piece of knitting which is worked at right angles to the first.

Flat edgings

The first square shown here represents any piece of knitting, in any stitch. The second diagram shows the same piece of knitting with an extra strip knitted on. The extra piece is in the same stitch, but knitted in a different direction.

 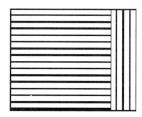

Measure the length of the edge where you need to pick up the stitches. If possible, do this by counting the number of rows as the edge may have stretched. You also need to know your tension. The direction that was the rows originally will now be stitches and the stitches will be the rows.

When you pick up the stitches, you will be working into the row ends of the original piece. If the tension is two stitches and three rows to a centimetre, you must pick up two stitches from the ends of three rows. This means that you should pick up a stitch from the first row end and another from the second, ignore the third, then pick up again from the fourth and fifth and ignore the sixth. Work all along in the same way.

Similarly, in a different stitch, which gives a much wider piece of knitting, the tension might be three stitches and two rows to a centimetre. This time you need to pick up three stitches from every two row ends. Because you need more stitches than there are row ends, you will have to pick up extra stitches between them, or make extra stitches.

The easiest stitch to work with is garter stitch. One stitch is picked up from the end of each ridge (two rows) of the knitting.

These rules apply when you are using the same stitch, needles and yarn and you want the extra piece to lie flat. On the following pages you will find out how to pick up the right number of stitches with mathematical precision, when your tension does not work out to such obvious numbers. These methods are not suitable for a band which has to pull in the edge of a garment to make it tighter, or for the edge of a shaped piece of knitting, or where the new piece has to flare out from the old one.

Ribbing

If your bands are to be in ribbing, or any other different stitch, you really need another tension square to establish the exact number of stitches needed. Rib is always narrower than the same number of stitches in stocking stitch. The extent to which it pulls in will depend on the type of rib used, the yarn and the size of needles. The depth of the rib also affects how much it pulls in. A few rows will still be being partly stretched by the main part of the knitting, whereas a deep rib will be able to pull in more.

The position of a rib will determine how much you want it to draw in the knitting. Round the lower edge of a garment you may want only slight gathering, or you may want a very bloused effect. The neckline usually stays fairly flat. The sleeve cuffs will probably need to come in quite a lot to stop them flapping over your hands. Either work out the tension for a piece of rib, or start with a piece which is less crucial and use this to establish how big the others need to be.

Where you want an edge to flare out, think about how much extra you need and add stitches accordingly. If you want a very frilly edge, twice as far round as the original, increase on every stitch so that you have twice as many stitches as you started with. The first few rows of this will look rather wrinkled. You will need to knit several more rows before the fullness becomes obvious. If you need less fullness, add fewer stitches. For example, if the frill is to be 10% bigger than before, increase on every tenth stitch. The amount you need to add will vary according to what you are making. It could be a very full frill round a child's dress, or a peplum on the bottom of a jacket, which would need to be big enough to go over the hips, or a slightly floppy brim for a hat.

Evenly spaced picking up

From your tension: divide the rows by what you get when you take the stitches away from the rows. If the answer is a decimal, round to the nearest whole number. An answer of 3 means miss out every third row end. If the answer is 4, miss out every fourth row end, etc.

Example

1.7 stitches and 3 rows to 1cm.

$$\begin{aligned} & (rows) \quad divided\ by \quad (rows - stitches) \\ =\ & (3) \quad divided\ by \quad (3 - 1.7) \\ =\ & 3 \quad divided\ by \quad 1.3 \\ =\ & 2.3076923,\ which\ rounds\ down\ to\ 2 \end{aligned}$$

You need to miss out every second row end.

This is not completely accurate, because of the rounding down. You can be more accurate by rounding to the nearest half row.

In this example that would be 2.5. In reality you cannot miss out one row end in every 2.5 rows, but you can miss out 2 in every 5. This is still not completely accurate, but should be close enough for most practical purposes. If you want to be more accurate still, you will need to add an occasional extra stitch if you rounded up, or miss one if you rounded down.

Negative answers

Using this rule with a tension of 2.4 rows and 3 stitches to one centimetre gives an answer of -4.

A minus answer shows that you need to make extra stitches. With an answer of -4, after every fourth row end you must make a new stitch without going into a row end.

Garter stitch

Two stitches and four rows to the centimetre is a typical garter stitch tension, and when you follow the rules for calculating picking up stitches, it gives an answer of exactly 2.

Garter stitch should always give an answer of 2, whatever yarn you are using, because there are always twice as many rows as stitches to make a square. The 2 means that you should miss picking up a stitch at the end of every second (alternate) row. In garter stitch 2 rows make one ridge, so each ridge has a row where you do pick up a stitch and a row where you do not. If you pick up one stitch from each ridge, you will automatically be missing out alternate rows.

The rules work in exactly the same way whether you decide to work in centimetres, inches, or some other measurement, as long as you use the same measurements for everything. If you change any of the elements of the original piece, the new one will not be flat. Smaller needles, or thinner yarn, will pull it in. Thicker needles or yarn will have the opposite effect. Changing the stitch can make differences in either direction, depending on the stitch chosen. You can also deliberately alter the appearance by picking up more, or less, than the calculated number of stitches.

14
Placing a design

When you have mastered the basic techniques of designing your own knitwear, you will soon become bored with knitting plain garments and start experimenting with pattern.

The words pattern and design can cause a great deal of confusion. From now on, when I use the word pattern I am referring to some sort of picture or decorative finish, not a set of instructions such as those on a commercial pattern.

You can take a picture from any commercial pattern (or elsewhere) and use it on your own garment. If the picture is designed for knitwear, it can almost certainly be used on any other knitted garment. The tension may be different, but the proportions of the stitches are not likely to vary enough to make any noticeable difference. Do not use designs intended for cross stitch work, or anything else based on a square grid. Knitted stitches are not square and the picture will look flattened.

If you would like to create your own patterns and pictures, you can buy special knitters' graph paper, with rectangles in the correct proportion. Learn to use existing patterns before you move on to this stage.

Pictures

When you have found a picture you want to use, you need to compare the number of stitches and rows it covers with the number of stitches and rows you have available.

Is the picture the size you want? If the answer is no, you should probably look for another. Rescaling a picture is extremely difficult and needs very thorough planning and calculation, as well as a certain amount of artistic talent! It is outside the scope of this book, which deals with simple calculations only.

Note

If you are working on a knitting machine, this is the first time you will not be using the same instructions as the hand-knitter. Remember that you are working from the back of your pieces and everything is reversed when you look at it from the other side.

Example

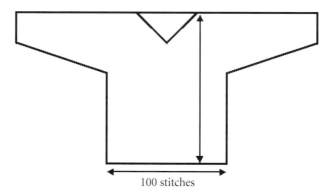

100 stitches

35 stitches

If your sweater is 100 stitches wide and the picture is only 35 stitches, you may think it is rather small for the sweater. You have several choices.

1 Use the picture twice.

In this example you could leave 10 stitches before you begin working from the rectangular chart of the picture. Leave 10 stitches then work the chart again. This leaves another 10 stitches at the other side.

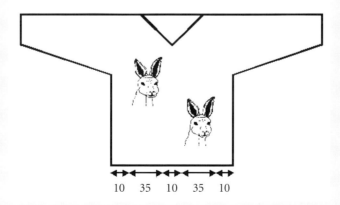

10   35   10   35   10

The two pictures are not knitted at the same time, as one is higher up than the other. Decide how far up you want the *bottom of each to be. In the example, the bottom of the second picture is started before the top of the first one is finished.*

2 Make the picture twice (or three times, if it fits) the original size.

Double the dimensions of the drawing and knit two stitches and two rows for every one on the original. In the example the new picture will be 70 stitches wide. This leaves 30 stitches across the sweater which are not needed for the picture. If you want the picture to be in the centre, leave 15 at each side.

This method of enlarging means that every stitch turns into a block of four and you could find the result of this unpleasant, because it might give a jagged edge to your picture. You may be able to make some refinements as you knit, to smooth out the curves, but this will have to be a matter for your artistic judgement.

Repeat patterns

Many designs consist of a pattern which repeats several times around the garment. This could be a stitch pattern worked in a single colour or a multi-coloured design.

If you are intending to use a stitch from a book of stitch patterns, you will probably find instructions that tell you the multiple of stitches to use.

The simplest would say 'multiples of 2'. A knit one, purl one rib is an example of this, where you knit one stitch and purl the next all the way across the row.

KPKPKPKPKP   This has 5 pattern repeats, making 10 stitches in all.

If you wanted both ends of the row to be the same, you would have to end on a knit stitch, not purl. Because you need an extra stitch, the instructions would be 'multiples of 2, plus 1'. This means you should work out the multiples first, then add an extra stitch.

KPKPKPKPKPK   This has 5 pattern repeats and an extra stitch, making 11 stitches in all.

Larger repeats work in exactly the same way. It is unlikely that you will have exactly the right number of stitches available, so you will need to adjust.

Divide the number of stitches you want by the multiple. You will probably get an answer with a decimal and have to decide whether to go to the number below and have a very slightly smaller garment, or whether to go to the number above and end up with something slightly larger. If there is a 'plus x' in the instructions, you should also take that into account.

Before you decide which of these options to choose, work out the exact number of stitches for both the larger and smaller numbers. Multiply the numbers by the multiple, add on the 'plus x', then you can make your decision.

With some patterns, particularly multi-coloured, continuous designs, it is important to take into account any stitches which might disappear into seams and add any extras required.

If the design you are using is not continuous, you may be able to solve the problems by allowing more, or fewer, stitches between the repeats.

It is vital to plan carefully so that you start with the right number of stitches.

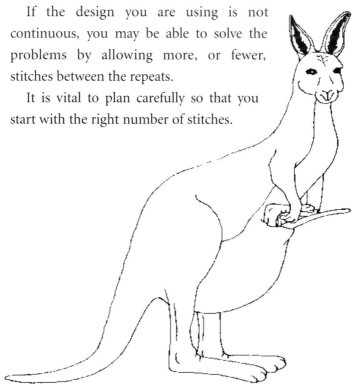

Conclusion

This book will not help you to decide which colour or type of yarn to choose, or what style will suit you, but you should now be able to plan the making of a simple sweater, jacket or cardigan. You do not have to start from scratch and design the whole thing yourself, although you do now have all the information to enable you to do so. You may only want to adapt existing patterns to make them fit better, or change the shape of the sleeve, or move the decoration to a different position. You can do all that – and much more.

The calculations are not difficult if you think about what you are doing and tackle the problem in stages. Everyone makes mistakes sometimes, so do not be content to rely on that first set of calculations. Keep checking to make sure everything is coming out as it should. If you have made a mistake, it is better to find out early on than finish the garment and find it does not fit. The most important thing is to take the plunge and have a go at working it all out. You will be amazed at what you can create.

Part Three
Project

15
V-neck Cardigan

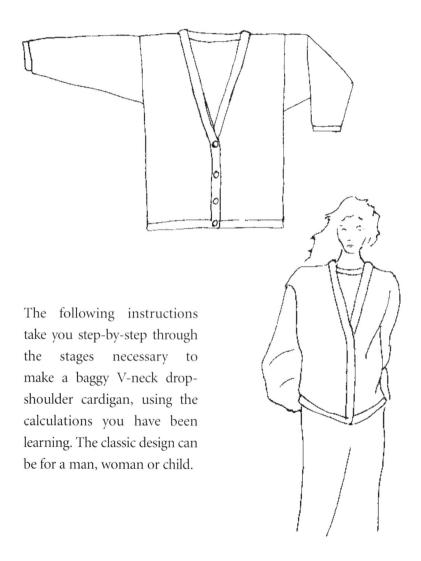

The following instructions take you step-by-step through the stages necessary to make a baggy V-neck drop-shoulder cardigan, using the calculations you have been learning. The classic design can be for a man, woman or child.

Measurements

Find a garment that fits you well and try it on to see how it compares with the garment you want to make. It does not have to be a cardigan. Note any alterations you would like. These might be the length of the body or sleeves, the depth of the armholes, the position of the V, etc. Take off the garment, lay it flat on the floor or table and fasten any buttons.

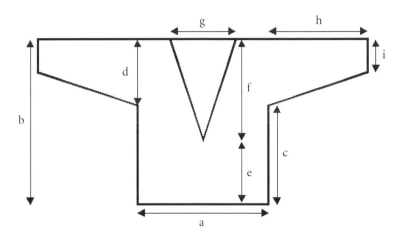

Use a good, firm tape to take the measurements shown in the diagram, remembering to add or subtract any changes you have decided to make. None of the bands is shown on the diagram. If your garment has bands or ribs, measure as though they were not there. They can be added to the new garment later. If they distort the normal shape of the garment, try to spread it as flat as possible while measuring.

Decide now whether to work in centimetres or inches and stick to your chosen units throughout the project.

		cm	or	in
a	**Width**	————		————
b	**Length**	————		————
c	**Length to armhole**	————		————
d	**Depth of armhole**	————		————
e	**Length to bottom of neck**	————		————
f	**Depth of neck**	————		————
g	**Width of neck**	————		————
h	**Length of sleeve**	————		————
i	**Width of bottom of sleeve**	————		————

Some of these measurements will not be needed for this project, but they can be used to check that you measured accurately. Add **c** and **d** and you should get **b** (the full length). Adding **e** and **f** should also give **b**.

Measurements **d** and **i** are only half that needed for the sleeve and will have to be doubled later.

If you prefer to fill in the measurements on a drawing, use the blank diagram shown here.

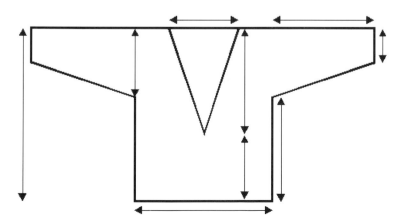

Tension

Make a piece of knitting using your chosen yarn, needles and stitch. The exact size is unimportant, but it must be bigger than 10cm (4in). The ball band will tell you the approximate number of stitches. The band will also give instructions on how the yarn should be treated, so follow these and prepare your piece in the same way that you will treat the finished pieces. Mark off a 10cm (4in) square as described on pages 10–11.

Count stitches and rows

Stitches across square _____   Rows in square _____

Calculate tension

Stitch tension
Divide stitches by 10 _____ (cm)
or
Divide stitches by 4 _____ (in)

Row tension
Divide rows by 10 _____ (cm)
or
Divide rows by 4 _____ (in)

b

a

The back

Number of stitches = **a** x stitch tension
= _____

Number of rows = **b** x row tension
= _____

If you want to start with a rib, use the same number of stitches you have calculated for the back. This will hold the lower edge in a little, but will not pull in the baggy shape too much.

To knit the back

Cast on the number of stitches calculated. Knit the rib (if required) on smaller needles. Change to the correct size of needles for the main part and knit the number of rows calculated. Cast off.

The fronts

Straight section

Number of stitches $\qquad$ = ½ (**a** x stitch tension)

= _____

Number of rows to start of neck

= **e** x row tension

= _____

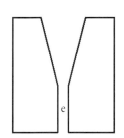

Neck shaping – width

Number of stitches (**j**) = ½ (**g** x stitch tension)

= _____

Neck shaping – length

Number of rows (**k**) = **f** x row tension

= _____

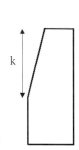

Calculate frequency of decrease (simple method)

k divided by **j** = every _____ rows

(Ignore any numbers after the decimal point in this answer.)

To knit the fronts

Cast on the number of stitches for the straight section. Knit the rib to match the back. Knit the number of rows in the straight section to the start of the neck. Knit the number of rows in **k**, decreasing one stitch at the neck edge with the frequency calculated until the **j** decreases have been worked. (Using this simple calculation method there may be a few rows near the top which have no shaping.)

Knit the other front to match. The neck shaping will be at the opposite side to make a matching pair.

The sleeves

Number of rows = **h** x row tension

= _____

Number of stitches – bottom (**l**) = 2 x **i** x stitch tension

= _____

Number of stitches – top (**m**) = 2 x **d** x stitch tension

= _____

Stitches to be increased = **m** – **l**

Pairs of stitches to be increased = ½ (**m** – **l**)

= _____

Calculate frequency of increase (simple method)

Number of rows divided by pairs of increases = every _____ rows (Ignore any numbers after the decimal point in this answer.)

Rib

If you want to begin the sleeves with a rib, use the rib you knitted for the back to find the number of stitches to fit over your hand. Make a circle which fits and count how many stitches are in the circle. After the rib, increase to get the correct number of stitches for the bottom of the sleeve. This is a difficult calculation, so refer back to Getting the Stitches You Want (page 63). It is much easier to add the rib later.

To knit the sleeves

Cast on the number of stitches for the bottom. Increase at both ends of the rows calculated for the frequency, until you have the number of stitches needed for the top. Knit straight until you have the number of rows calculated for the length.

Making up

Joining main pieces

Join the fronts to the back at the shoulder. Mark the position for the top of the sleeve on the front and back, then stitch this in place, taking care to place the centre of the sleeve at the shoulder seam. Join the side seams.

Lower edging

If you have not already knitted an edging for the bottom, pick up stitches all along the front, back and second front, and knit the edging in one piece. Cast off very loosely.

Sleeve finishing

If you have not already knitted the edgings for the sleeves, use your lower edging to decide how many stitches will go over your hand and pick up that number evenly along the lower edge of the sleeve. Knit the edging and cast off very loosely. Stitch the sleeve seams.

Front bands (simple method)

Use your back edging to decide how many stitches will give the right width for the band. Knit a long strip to go up the front and round the neck until it reaches the centre back. This is the button band. Stitch it onto the cardigan and stitch the buttons onto it in the positions you require. Count the number of rows to each button.

Knit a second band for the other side, inserting a buttonhole in the position of each of the buttons. Stitch the band to the cardigan.

Refinements

This project has used some of the simplest methods available to produce a very basic garment. Once you have gained confidence in these methods, you can move on to more ambitious projects and let your imagination take over. On the next page you will find a blank shape which you can use for the measurements for your own projects. It may not look much like the shape you are aiming to create: your planned garment may be longer, shorter, or more shaped. The diagram is merely to remind you of what needs to be measured and calculated. You could draw your own if you prefer. Annotate any drawing in the way you find most helpful. The right way is the way that works best for you.

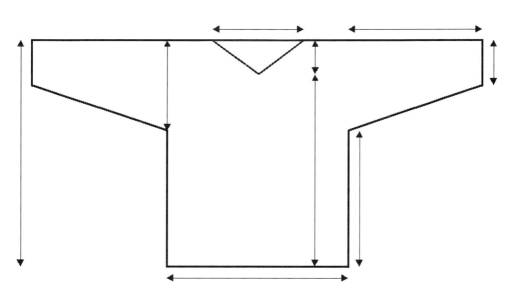

Measurements

	cm	or	in
Width	_____		_____
Length	_____		_____
Length to armhole	_____		_____
Depth of armhole	_____		_____
Length to bottom of neck	_____		_____
Depth of neck	_____		_____
Width of neck	_____		_____
Length of sleeve	_____		_____
Width of bottom of sleeve	_____		_____

Appendix: Making a padded board

A padded board is extremely useful, the bigger the better, but think about where you will store it before you get carried away with the size. Mine is plenty big enough to hold the back of an average-sized sweater or jacket. It measures about 75 x 65cm.

Make it from any wood which will not warp and cover it with several thicknesses of padding. It should be able to hold pins and withstand them being moved many times. It should also be able to stand being sprayed with water, steamed or ironed. Some types of foam would not be suitable, as they might melt under the iron. Thick old blankets make good, sturdy padding.

The outer cover should be a smooth pure cotton. Man-made fibres will create static and your knitting may cling. The ideal fabric is some sort of check marked out in centimetre or inch squares so that you can also use it as a ready-made grid. Mine is black and white gingham in centimetre squares, which makes it very easy to count out the number of squares in any project.

Make the padding larger than the board, pull it round to the back, cut away all the double thicknesses at the corners and staple or tack it into place. Do not rely on the cover to hold the padding. It will eventually wrinkle up underneath.

Make the cotton cover larger than the padding. Pull it round to the back, mitring the corners before you fasten it down. Do not cut away the excess fabric or it may start to fray. It is also advisable to fold in the edge of the fabric so you are stapling through a double thickness. There will be a good deal of strain on the fabric.

I have two loop handles on the back of my board. They are simply loops of strong tape, stapled into place. They are useful for carrying the board, because it can be awkward to grip.

A makeshift board for measuring a small sample can be made from a block of polystyrene, or even a polystyrene tile. This will eventually start to break up when pins are pushed into it, but it is cheap and easy to replace. It can also have lines marked on it for a particular project, after which it can be thrown away.

About the authors

Pat Ashforth and Steve Plummer are both mathematics teachers. Pat is Assistant Head of Maths at Denbigh High School in Luton, and Steve is Head of Maths at Walton High School, Nelson, in Lancashire. A lifelong knitter, Pat became increasingly interested in experimenting with design and in finding simple mathematical rules which anyone could follow to create original garments. She and Steve then worked together to explain and illustrate these principles in the two books *Creating Knitwear Designs* and *Making Knitwear Fit*. They have written one previous book together, called *Woolly Thoughts*.

BOOKS

WOODTURNING

dventures in Woodturning	*David Springett*	Pleasure & Profit from Woodturning	*Reg Sherwin*
ert Marsh: Woodturner	*Bert Marsh*	Practical Tips for Turners & Carvers	*GMC Publications*
ll Jones' Notes from the Turning Shop	*Bill Jones*	Practical Tips for Woodturners	*GMC Publications*
arving on Turning	*Chris Pye*	Spindle Turning	*GMC Publications*
olouring Techniques for Woodturners	*Jan Sanders*	Turning Miniatures in Wood	*John Sainsbury*
ecorative Techniques for Woodturners	*Hilary Bowen*	Turning Wooden Toys	*Terry Lawrence*
ceplate Turning: Features, Projects, Practice	*GMC Publications*	Useful Woodturning Projects	*GMC Publications*
reen Woodwork	*Mike Abbott*	Woodturning: A Foundation Course	*Keith Rowley*
ustrated Woodturning Techniques	*John Hunnex*	Woodturning Jewellery	*Hilary Bowen*
eith Rowley's Woodturning Projects	*Keith Rowley*	Woodturning Masterclass	*Tony Boase*
ake Money from Woodturning	*Ann & Bob Phillips*	Woodturning: A Source Book of Shapes	*John Hunnex*
ulti-Centre Woodturning	*Ray Hopper*	Woodturning Techniques	*GMC Publications*
		Woodturning Wizardry	*David Springett*

WOODCARVING

he Art of the Woodcarver	*GMC Publications*	Wildfowl Carving Volume 1	*Jim Pearce*
arving Birds & Beasts	*GMC Publications*	Wildfowl Carving Volume 2	*Jim Pearce*
arving Realistic Birds	*David Tippey*	Woodcarving: A Complete Course	*Ron Butterfield*
arving on Turning	*Chris Pye*	Woodcarving for Beginners: Projects, Techniques & Tools	
ecorative Woodcarving	*Jeremy Williams*		*GMC Publications*
ractical Tips for Turners & Carvers	*GMC Publications*	Woodcarving Tools, Materials & Equipment	*Chris Pye*

PLANS, PROJECTS, TOOLS & THE WORKSHOP

More Woodworking Plans & Projects	*GMC Publications*	Sharpening: The Complete Guide	*Jim Kingshott*
ectric Woodwork: Power Tool Woodworking	*Jeremy Broun*	Sharpening Pocket Reference Book	*Jim Kingshott*
he Incredible Router	*Jeremy Broun*	Woodworking Plans & Projects	*GMC Publications*
aking & Modifying Woodworking Tools	*Jim Kingshott*	The Workshop	*Jim Kingshott*

TOYS & MINIATURES

esigning & Making Wooden Toys	*Terry Kelly*	Making Wooden Toys & Games	*Jeff & Jennie Loader*
eraldic Miniature Knights	*Peter Greenhill*	Miniature Needlepoint Carpets	*Janet Granger*
aking Board, Peg & Dice Games	*Jeff & Jennie Loader*	Restoring Rocking Horses	*Clive Green & Anthony Dew*
aking Little Boxes from Wood	*John Bennett*	Turning Miniatures in Wood	*John Sainsbury*
aking Unusual Miniatures	*Graham Spalding*	Turning Wooden Toys	*Terry Lawrence*

CREATIVE CRAFTS

he Complete Pyrography	*Stephen Poole*	Creating Knitwear Designs	*Pat Ashforth & Steve Plummer*
ross Stitch on Colour	*Sheena Rogers*	Making Knitwear Fit	*Pat Ashforth & Steve Plummer*
mbroidery Tips & Hints	*Harold Hayes*	Miniature Needlepoint Carpets	*Janet Granger*
		Tatting Collage	*Lindsay Rogers*

UPHOLSTERY AND FURNITURE

DOLLS' HOUSES & DOLLS' HOUSE FURNITURE

OTHER BOOKS

VIDEOS

MAGAZINES

WOODTURNING ● WOODCARVING ● BUSINESSMATTERS

The above represents a full list of all titles currently published or scheduled to be published. All are available direct from the Publishers or through bookshops, newsagents and specialist retailers. To place an order, or to obtain a complete catalogue, contact

GMC Publications, 166 High Street, Lewes, East Sussex BN7 1XU United Kingdom
Tel: 01273 488005 Fax: 01273 478606

Orders by credit card are accepted